Introduction

The area covered by this guide is one of the most popular walking districts in Scotland, and its hills, lochs, glens and woodlands provide an enormous range of routes within a small area.

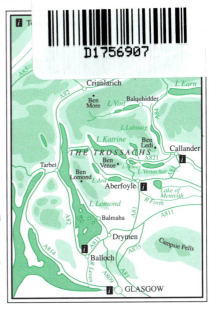

At the heart of the area are The Trossachs. The exact extent of 'The Trossachs' is difficult to define: the original Gaelic seems to have been a reference to the short glen between Loch Achray and Loch Katrine, including the flanking hills of Ben A'an and Ben Venue. But over time the term has spread in its geographical extent, and now covers the whole area between Loch Lomond in the west, Callander in the east, Aberfoyle in the south and Balquhidder in the north.

The area is a mass of hills – of moderate height but dramatic in appearance – separated by winding glens and long, narrow lochs. The walks in this area tend, therefore, to be hill climbs (the short steep ascent of Ben A'an *(Walk 20)*, the longer climbs up Ben Ledi *(15)* and Ben Venue *(22))* and paths along glens (the paths to Falls of Leny *(16)* and up Glen Finglas *(19))* and by lochs (Loch Ard *(27)*, Loch Katrine *(21))*. In addition, Forestry Commission Scotland (FCS) have planted several conifer forests in the area, which include numerous car parks and waymarked paths *(11,13,23.25,26,27)*.

The popularity and romantic image of The Trossachs is due largely to the work of Sir Walter Scott. The poet and novelist made many visits to the area (often staying at Aberfoyle), and made use of the area's landscape and history in some of his early works: notably his early ballad-epic *The Lady of the Lake* (1810), which was largely set around Loch Katrine. This work was largely responsible for the creation of Highland tourism in the 19th century, leading to the growth of villages such as Aberfoyle *(25,26)* and Callander *(16,17)*, and of the little settlement at Brig o' Turk *(18)*, in the heart of the glen which gave its name to the area. Visitors to Loch Katrine will note that the steamer which operates on the loch is called the *Sir Walter Scott*.

The Lady of the Lake was whimsy, but Scott did include genuine historical characters his work. In 1817 he published the novel *Rob Roy*, the eponymous hero of which – Rob Roy MacGregor (c. 1660-1740) – is indelibly associated with The Trossachs. Though essentially a rural racketeer, Rob Roy's independence, and his quick-wittedness in his tussles with authority, have made him a lasting folk hero. Walkers will come across numerous references to him throughout the area, including his birthplace at Glengyle *(21)*, his home at Inverlochlarig *(9)*, various caves where he is said to have hidden from his pursuers *(28)* and his grave at Balquhidder *(10,11,12)*.

To the west of The Trossachs is Loch Lomond: the largest inland water in Great Britain. The loch is around 24 miles (38km) long; narrow at its northern end and broad at the south, where it is dotted with wooded islands *(32)*. At

the southern end of the loch is Balloch *(37)*, which is now home to Lomond Shores: The National Park Gateway Centre (Loch Lomond & The Trossachs National Park was established in 2002). With the exception of Walks 4 and 38, all the routes in this book fall within the boundaries of the National Park.

The main road runs up the western side of the loch (not included in this guide). Access to the eastern shore is less easy.

Drumkinnon Tower at Loch Lomond Shores

There is a narrow public road (often busy in the summer) running north from Drymen, through the little resort of Balmaha *(30,31,32,33)* and on up the wooded shore to end at the hotel and car park at Rowardennan (the start of the path up Ben Lomond: the splendid Munro which dominates the eastern side of the loch *(36)*). North from this, the loch can only be reached by car by following the narrow road west from Aberfoyle to the hotel at Inversnaid *(28)*.

Falls of Dochart, Killin (see Walk 7)

Having said this, access is simple enough on foot: the West Highland Way *(39)* – the long-distance footpath linking Glasgow and Fort William – runs up the eastern shore of the loch before continuing north *via* Crianlarich and Tyndrum. If you simply wish a good view of the loch, short climbs will lead to fine views from Craigie Fort *(31)* and Conic Hill *(30)* to the east, and from Duncryne *(29)* and The Whangie *(38)* to the south.

North of The Trossachs and Loch Lomond is Breadalbane. Like The Trossachs this is a hilly area, but it is built on a grander scale. The glens (notably Glen Dochart and Glen Lochay, which feed Loch Tay) are longer and broader; the hills higher and more rugged. Of the hills in the area covered by this book, only one peak south of the northern end of Loch Lomond (Ben Lomond) is a Munro (a peak over 3,000 feet). North of this there are several, including the fine double peak of Ben More and Stob Binnein *(3)* and An Caisteal *(2)*. An investigation of the Ordnance Survey maps will suggest many possible routes for keen mountain walkers, but there are also shorter walks available, notably the three short walks around the village of Killin, at the foot of Loch Tay *(5,6,7)* (the views from Creag Bhuidhe are particularly fine) and the short, steep climb to the mines above Tyndrum *(1)*.

In short, this is a splendid area for walking of all types.

The SS Sir Walter Scott *on Loch Katrine* (see Walk 21)

A short, steep climb to view the remains of old lead mine workings above the village of Tyndrum. Great views over Glen Lochy and Strath Fillan. The route crosses old spoil heaps, so the going is rough and slippy in places. Length: 2¹/₂ miles/4km (there and back); Height Climbed: 1000ft/300m.

O.S. Sheet 50

The village of Tyndrum lies at the junction of the A82 and A85. It is on the West Highland Way (*see* Walk 39) so is geared up for walkers.

Start from Tyndrum Lower train station (follow the signs from the main road) where there is a car park. Go through the kissing gate and cross the railway line (carefully). On the other side, turn right onto a path that leads off the main track and runs, initially, alongside the railway line.

The path soon cuts into the woods and continues until you reach a wide stream bed (at this point a path cuts off to the right: make a note of this for your return route). Cross the stream-bed and continue a little further; watching for the remains of a small open mine to your left. Carefully climb the faint path to the left of this to join a larger path which leads straight up to the spoil heaps. Follow

this path up through these impressive mounds of broken rock, being careful not to cross the safety fence to your left. The path becomes fainter and more difficult to follow as it zig-zags up the slope, but it continues as far as the watershed above the mines. From here there is a splendid view of the surrounding mountains, including Ben Lui to the south-west.

You should descend by the same path (carefully), but when you reach the far side of the stream bed, instead of following the outward route turn left, under the railway line. A waymarked path starts on the far side, leading back towards Tyndrum. When you reach the houses, you have a choice. A turn to the left will lead to the Green Welly Stop, at the north end of the village (a good place for refreshments); a turn to the right will lead back to the car park.

An Caisteal ('The Castle') is a beautiful top just south of Crianlarich. It is a Munro and there is no clear path up it for much of the way, so this walk is for experienced hill walkers only. This is a strenuous expedition that requires good navigation skills. Length: **8 miles/13km** *(full circuit); Height Climbed:* **2600ft/800m.**

Drive south from Crianlarich on the A82 Glasgow road. After a little over a mile park in a large lay-by to the left (east) of the road.

Cross a stile at the north end of the lay-by then cross a muddy field to a tunnel, visible ahead, where a landrover track passes under the railway. Pass through this, cross the bridge over the River Falloch beyond, and follow the clear track up the glen.

After a mile/1.5km the track passes through a gate in a fence. Turn right here and follow the line of the fence – the ground is wet in places, but there is no doubt about the route.

Pass a small wooden gate in the fence and continue climbing to a larger, metal gate. Turn left here and start climbing. There is no path on this section: just go straight up the steep slope of Sròn Gharbh until you reach the top. The views are superb.

South from Sròn Gharbh there is a clear path along the ridge of Twistin Hill, leading all the way to the rocky summit of An Caisteal. Here you have a choice. For the shortest return, simply retrace your steps. If you wish to extend your walk, follow the steep, rocky path which drops to the bealach between An Casiteal and Beinn a' Chroin. Turn left (north-east) from

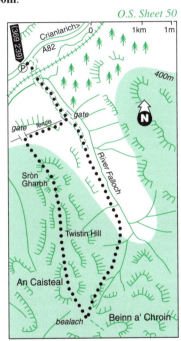

O.S. Sheet 50

the lowest point of the bealach and follow the left-hand side of the burn down into the glen. There is no path at first, it is wet and there are some burns to cross, but it is a pleasant glen and you eventually join the end of the track on which you started.

*These two hills dominate the skyline south of Glen Dochart and are traditionally climbed together. The views from the summits are spectacular but care should be taken on the early stages of the walk where there is no obvious path. Length: **7 miles/11km**; Total Height Climbed: **4255ft/1297m**. Experienced walkers could extended this walk to take in more of the peaks along the ridge.*

O.S. Sheet 51

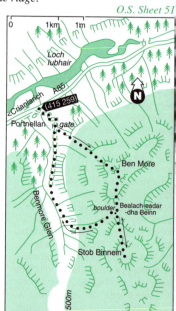

The walk starts from a broad gravel verge 2 miles east of Crianlarich on the A85; to the south of the road just beyond the buildings at Portnellan. Park here and follow the signposted path up the embankment and over a stile to join a farm track. Turn left along this, winding up the hill to pass through a gate in a fence.

Once through the gate, you need to leave the track and head directly up the steep slope of Ben More. There is no path on the early part of the climb – everyone chooses their own route – just aim for the apparent peak. You should eventually pick up a rough path which leads to the summit.

Rest for a while at the summit, enjoying the stunning panoramic views. To the south is Stob Binnein: the next peak along the ridge. To reach it, descend steeply to Bealach-eadar-dha Beinn, the col between the two hills. Note the obvious boulder on the bealach (the start point for the return route). Cross the bealach and climb the rough, clear path to the summit of Stob Binnein.

From the summit, experienced walkers may choose to continue to other peaks. For this route, however, return to the bealach by the same path

and, instead of re-climbing Ben More, follow a faint path (west) down the left-hand side of a small burn into Benmore Glen. Swing right to join a clearer path by the Benmore Burn. This eventually joins the end of the farm track which you started on. Follow this back to the start.

*This steep, lineal walk climbs a small glen to the remains of several
abandoned settlements, and has a real wilderness feel to it. There is a
good path on the route described, but higher up the path disappears.
For hillwalkers, the walk provides access to the surrounding peaks.
Length:* **2 miles/3km** *(there and back); Height Climbed:* **650ft/200m**.

From the centre of Killin, follow
the A827 north. On the edge of the
village is the Bridge of Lochay Hotel,
with the bridge just beyond. Cross
this and turn left onto a single-track
road. Follow this as it winds up
the glen. After 3 miles you pass a
farmhouse and cross a bridge over a
large burn coming down from your
right. Just beyond there is a gate on
your right and a small 'Hill Phones'
box. Park in a large lay-by a little
further down the road.

Walk back to the gate and follow
the muddy track beyond. This leads
you through another gate, then up into
a field where you will find the first
– and most complete – of the ruined
settlements.

The track disappears in the field,
but there is a large stile over the dyke
at the top, and from there the way is
obvious again; following a clear track
up to the low, broken walls of a group
of shielings.

This is the end of the easy walking
and a good place to turn back. There
are more ruins further up the glen,
but if you wish to continue you will
need to cross a burn coming down
from Meall Ghaordaidh, just beyond
the shielings (this could be fairly
difficult in wet conditions). The path

O.S. Sheet 51

continues on the other side of the
burn, heading up through some old
gateposts, but from this point onwards
it becomes broken and finally
disappears.

5 Creag Bhuidhe / 6 The Old Railway /
7 Achmore Wood ⸻⸻⸻⸻ B/C/C

Three walks of varying degrees of difficulty starting from Killin. **5)** *A challenging climb leading to rewarding views over Loch Tay and the surrounding countryside. Length:* **2¹/₂ miles/4km** *(there and back); Height Climbed:* **1100ft/340m.** **6)** *A short, flat, varied walk, starting on a former railway line and returning by the loch/river bank. Damp in places; wellingtons advised. Length:* **1¹/₂ miles/2.5km**; *Height Climbed:* negligible. **7)** *A pleasant walk going out on a forest track and returning on a quiet public road. Length:* **2¹/₂ miles/4km**; *Height Climbed:* negligible.

O.S. Sheet 51

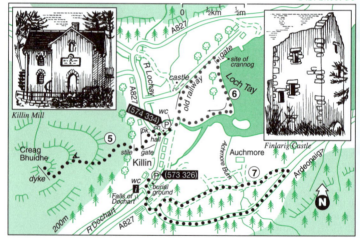

Walks 5 & 6) Driving north from the centre of Killin on the A827 there is a car park sign on the right, just before a church on the corner. The car park is a short way down the side road.

Walk 5) Walk back to the church, cross the main road, turn right past the McLaren Hall then left into a park. Walk up to the top left corner of the park and go through a pedestrian gate.

Climb the field beyond, looking for the stile which gives access to a band of oak wood. Already there are fine views of Killin and the surrounding countryside.

Go right beyond the stile and follow the steep, well-trodden path, through the wood and out onto open hillside. The path continues, rough but clear, and there are alternate flat and steep sections right to the top of the hill. As you near the top the path joins a dyke. Turn right along this, passing a large cairn shortly before reaching the summit. The views from the top are spectacular.

The best descent is to retrace your steps – taking care on the steepest sections, which are like stairs cut into the hillside. The alternative descent, heading for Glen Dochart and following the deer fence downhill is difficult underfoot and unrewarding.

Walk 6) Park in the same car park, but this time walk past the toilets and turn left along the old railway track.

Cross the bridge over the River Lochay and continue along the raised track. To your left, on a small hill, you may be able to see the ruins of Finlarig Castle, a Campbell stronghold. If you wish to get closer, wait until the track joins the public road then double back a short distance (the ruin may be unstable and is visited at the walker's own risk).

Continue along the track until you reach a small parking place and a gate leading to the loch. Go through this

and follow the loch-side path, noting the low promontory – site of an ancient crannog (dwelling on a man-made island) – jutting into the loch.

The path now follows the coast of Loch Tay till it swings right by the River Lochay and heads back towards the railway line and the bridge over the river. Turn left to return to the car park.

Walk 7) There is a car park just north of the bridge over the Falls of Dochart, to the east of the road. Park here, walk back to the bridge and cross over, noting the falls and, to your left, the picturesque island burial ground of Clan MacNab.

Beyond the bridge take the second turn to the left, signposted for Ardeonaig. Follow the road through the line of the old railway then turn left onto the driveway signposted for Auchmore.

Just after crossing the Achmore Burn the track splits. Go right, on the path marked 'Tourist Trail'. This climbs gently, offering fine views of Loch Tay and Ben Lawers beyond.

At the end of this path you pop out onto a minor tarred road. Turn right and follow this back to Killin (being careful of occasional traffic).

View from Creag Bhuidhe: 1 *Meall Corranaich* **2** *An Stùc* **3** *Ben Lawers* **4** *Beinn Bhreac* **5** *Loch Tay*

The viaduct which once carried a section of the old railway north from Lochearnhead through Glen Ogle remains a dramatic landmark, visible from the road. This walk takes you along the disused track and over the viaduct, with an option of returning on rougher paths through the glen.
*Length: 5¹/₂ **miles/9km**; Height Climbed: **600ft/180m**. The railway walk can be extended in either direction (see Walk 40).*

O.S. Sheet 51

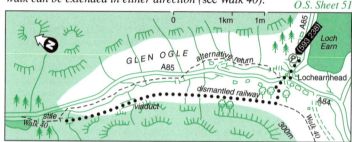

Start from Lochearnhead (the car park is by the A85, a short distance east of the junction with the A84) and walk back to the main road. Cross over (take care here) and turn right. The road passes between the stone piers of a dismantled railway bridge. Just beyond, a tarmac drive heads off to the left, signposted for the trail.

Turn onto this then turn right, almost immediately, on a rough path marked by a yellow arrow. Follow this for a short distance to a stile. Cross this and climb the steep path beyond to reach the old railway line.

Turn right. The old railway track is well surfaced, with curious small cattle-grids (for the cyclist) and signs marking the National Cycle Route 7 (part of the National Cycle Network). There are great views down over Glen Ogle and Loch Earn.

Follow the track across the old viaduct. A little beyond this a bridge crosses the line. Shortly before this there is a yellow arrow to the right, pointing to a stile.

The easiest – and driest – return from here is by the same route. If you would like to return by a different route, cross the stile and follow the rough path down into Glen Ogle.

The path (initially wet in places) starts along the old military road and is quite clear. Follow it, between the burn and the road, for a little over a mile/1.5km before crossing the road (carefully) and continuing, following the signposted way through the farmland and woodland to the east of the road. The path eventually crosses a footbridge over the burn then cuts across a muddy field to return to Lochearnhead.

9 Inverlochlarig

Inverlochlarig was one of the homes of Rob Roy MacGregor, who was doubtless attracted by its remoteness, and by the old paths leading over hill passes to north, south and west. This lineal walk follows a farm track along the bottom of the glen, and has great views of the surrounding hills. Length: up to **8 miles/13km** *(there and back); Height Climbed:* **350ft/110m**. *NB: this route provides access to some classic hill walks, but these should only be attempted by experienced hill walkers.*

O.S. Sheets 56 & 57

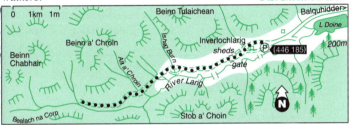

To reach Inverlochlarig, turn on to the Balquhidder road from the A84, two miles south of Lochearnhead. Follow this (mostly single-track and busy in summer) to its end (about 8 miles). At the road end there is a car park, a small sheltered picnic table and an information board.

Follow the private road that leads through the farm (the farm is built on the site of Rob Roy's house), over a bridge, and past large farm buildings on the right. Cross a stile by a gate and follow the track as far as you like. As you walk along, you will notice a bridge going over the river to your left – the access point for climbers to Stob a' Choin.

There are streams running over the track at a few points; generally they are small enough to be crossed easily,

though there are two exceptions. After 2 miles/3km the track reaches the Ishag Burn. A slight detour here leads to an estate bridge. The next large stream, Allt a' Chroin, has no bridge, and is impassible (or at least very difficult to cross) in wet weather.

If you come in dry weather, and manage to cross the stream, you will find the road ends quite abruptly about a mile/1.5km further on. Looking ahead, you get a good view of the pass of Bealach na Corp, leading into Glen Gyle (as the name implies, this was once a coffin route: a path along which bodies were carried on the way to burial).

For this walk, turn back here. Experienced climbers may note the faint path leading beyond this point up to Ben Chabhair.

10 **Creag an Tuirc** / 11 **Kirkton Glen** /
12 **Balquhidder to Ledcharrie** _____ C/B/A

Three walks of varying lengths in the hills behind Balquhidder. **10)** *A short, steep climb through woodland to a fine viewpoint associated with the Clan MacLaren. Length:* **2 miles/3km**; *Height Climbed:* **230ft/70m**. **11)** *A moderate Forestry Commission walk through conifer woodland, providing fine views of the surrounding hills. Length:* **5 miles/8km**; *Height Climbed:* **850ft/260m**. **12)** *A pleasant lineal hill crossing over an impressive little pass, with great views of the Glen Dochart hills. Unless you intend to walk there and back, it will be necessary to organise transport at the far end of the walk. Length:* **7 miles/11km** *(one way)*; *Height Climbed:* **1650ft/500m**.

O.S. Sheet 51

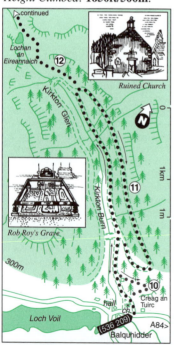

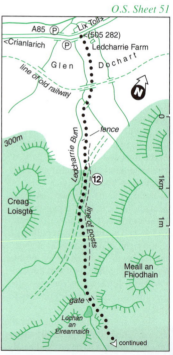

Balquhidder is the district name for the lands around Loch Voil. At the east end of the loch is a small settlement centred on two churches: one 17th-century and roofless; the other built in the mid-19th century. The area was historically associated with two clans, the MacLarens and the MacGregors, and the graves of the famous Rob Roy MacGregor and his family can be seen in the churchyard.

To reach the village, turn off the A84 about 2^1/$_2$ miles south of Lochearnhead on the road signposted for Balquhidder. The road leads back under the main road. Continue for about 2 miles to reach the church. Park either here or by the village hall.

For all three routes, start either at the signpost for the Ledcharrie path to the west of the church, or up the path to the east of the church. They soon join and are marked by a sign for the 'Kirkton Glen Walks'.

Climb up the clear track until there is a split, just beyond a building, with a yellow marker pointing to the right and a red marker straight ahead. Here you have a choice.

Walk 10) For the short climb up Creag an Tuirc ('Hill of the Boar'), turn right on the yellow route. The path is perfectly clear, leading up to a seat and a fine view up Loch Voil. The site is associated with the MacLarens, 'Creag an Tuirc' being the clan rallying cry.

Veer to the left when descending to join an alternative path down the hill.

Walks 11 & 12) For the longer walks, continue on the red route. The clear track continues up the right-hand side of the Kirkton Burn, with views of the surrounding hills gradually opening up.

At a crossroads beside a bridge over the burn, keep straight ahead following the red marker pole. The track then continues up the glen for a little over a mile/1.5km to a further junction near the end of the trees.

Walk 11) To complete the forest walk, turn right here (red post) down the eastern side of the glen. At the route's most southerly point there are fine views. From here the track cuts back to the junction by the burn.

Walk 12) At the junction at the top of the forest walk, look for a sign for the 'Glen Dochart Path'. The rough path winds uphill, crosses a stile, then heads up the last steep section to the pass, with its massive boulders. Just beyond are the restful shores of Lochan an Eireannaich.

If you don't have transport in Glen Dochart, turn back here. If you do, follow the faint path through a broken metal gate and on, downhill, to pick up a line of occasional fence posts. At one point the path merges with an ATV track for a short distance, before cutting off and continuing, straight down the valley, to reach the old railway line. Pass under this and continue to the A85 at Ledcharrie Farm.

To reach the northern end of the route: Drive 3 miles west of Lix Toll (the junction of the A827 and the A85) on the A85. Just beyond the turn off for Auchlyne (to the right), look for Ledcharrie Farm to the left and the lay-by just beyond. Park here and walk back to the farm.

A steep hill climb through conifers and over the open hill, with a possible alternative return. There are several ways up this hill, but the best route up is the marked forest walk. Length: **5 miles/8km** *(there and back); Height Climbed:* **1450ft/440m**. *Terrific views.*

O.S. Sheet 57

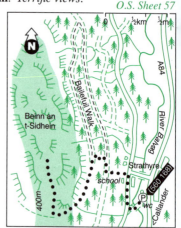

Start from the Forestry Commission car park at the south end of Strathyre, where there are toilets and information boards. At the back of the car park there are signs for the Beinn an t-Sidhein walk, which is a waymarked by blue markers. (NB: you will see the hill name – pronounced *ben sheean* – spelt a variety of ways.)

Follow the path to the left and across a bridge over the River Balvag. Just beyond this, take a path to your right, over a small footbridge. The path soon meets a single-track road. Follow this in the same direction, walking through the village. Shortly beyond the school you will see signs on your left for the waymarked walks.

The path leads up into the forest, climbing steeply to meet a forestry road. Follow the road to the right. Round the next corner, you will see a path leading up to your left, passing through a low stone wall. Follow this, zig-zagging steeply up the hill to join a clear forestry track.

A turn to the right at this point leads on to the Bailefuil Walk (green markers: this provides a possible alternative return route – *see* map). To continue the climb, however, turn left.

Follow this clear path across the face of the hill (ignoring paths cutting off to right and left) until it crosses a small stream near the edge of the conifer wood. The path passes through a fringe of young trees before looping round and up to a rocky outcrop.

The views from here are spectacular, looking south over Loch Lubnaig and west into Glen Buckie. (The actual summit of the hill is further north, but is quite flat and not really worth visiting.)

Take care while at the viewpoint; the path approaches by a safe route, but there is slippery grass above the cliffs on the east side. Return by the same route, or by the Bailefuil walk.

A lineal path between Loch Lubnaig and Loch Earn; steep at its southern end, but giving fine views. The route can be walked in either direction, though you will need to arrange transport at the far end. Length: **6 miles/9.5km** *(one way); Height Climbed:* **650ft/200m** *(either way). NB: Avoid this walk in spate conditions.*

O.S. Sheets 51 & 57

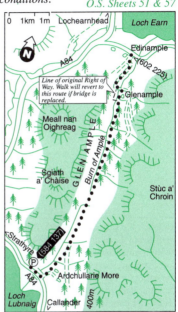

Park in the lay-by at Ardchullarie More, beside Loch Lubnaig on the A84, 5 miles north of Callander.

Head up the track signposted for Loch Earn. After 100m, turn left in front of outbuildings at a clear sign. Climb a narrow, steep path through trees to reach a forestry track. Turn left along this and continue climbing.

A gate, normally open, leads out of the forest onto the open hill. As you reach the top of the pass, about 1½ miles/2.5km from the start, the condition of the track deteriorates but the route is still clear.

On the level ground at the top, a steep and indistinct path heads off to the right (up Stùc a' Chroin). A little further along, a broad track heads off to the left through a gap in a dyke. This would take you to your destination, but it is much wetter so ignore it and keep on the path ahead.

You can now see Loch Earn and the hills beyond. Continue your descent to a forestry gate with an information board. From here, the track improves. Stay on the main track as it comes down to Glenample Farm. In this area, much damage was caused by the flash flood in 2004. The path is obliterated in places, although the way is still clear.

Just before the farm, arrows point left down towards the river. The old bridge was carried away by the flood, and until it is replaced the route goes down the east bank and crosses the river by the next bridge.

Continue down the track beyond to reach Edinample, on the south Loch Earn road.

A stiff lineal climb up one of the landmarks of the area – said to be visible from the ramparts of Edinburgh Castle. This is a Corbett – ie, over 2500ft/758m – and should not be attempted unless you are properly equipped. Length: **5 miles/8km** (there and back)*; Height Climbed:* **2500ft/760m**. *NB: There may be some restrictions on this path during forestry operations.*

O.S. Sheet 57

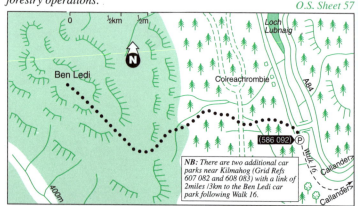

NB: There are two additional car parks near Kilmahog (Grid Refs 607 082 and 608 083) with a link of 2miles /3km to the Ben Ledi car park following Walk 16.

To reach the start of the climb, drive north from Callander on the A84 for about 3 miles and turn left at a sign for 'Strathyre Forest Cabins'. Cross the bailey bridge and turn left at the far end. Park in the car park here. (If the car park is full, there are two car parks near Kilmahog – *see* map). Watch out for cyclists! This is part of the cycle route from Callander to Lochearnhead. It is also the north end of Walk 16, if you wish to walk to the hill from Callander.

Form the car park, walk back to the end of the bridge and follow the clear, well-made path that climbs up through the forest. A possible translation of 'Ledi' is 'gentle slope', but this is not obvious until you have got up through the trees onto the south ridge. From here, it is relatively easy going to the summit.

The path is obvious, but go properly prepared and don't stray onto the steep eastern slope above Loch Lubnaig.

You may not be able to pick out Edinburgh Castle from the top, but on a clear day you should see the prominent Wallace Monument in Stirling and the Firth of Forth beyond. To the north and west the mountain panorama is dazzling.

Return the same way.

16 Callander to Falls of Leny   C

*This lineal walk follows a disused railway line (now a cycle route) to the impressive rapids at Falls of Leny. The Pass of Leny (the area around the falls) links the Highlands and Lowlands, and Queen Victoria likened its strategic importance to that of the Khyber Pass in India. Possibly an exaggeration, though the ruined Roman fort at Bochastle suggests the site did have military significance. Length: **3 miles/5km** (one way); Height Climbed: negligible. Possible link with Walk 15.*   *O.S. Sheet 57*

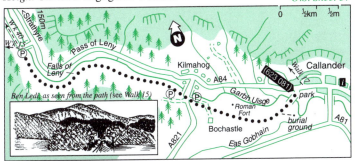

This walk starts from Callander town centre. Walk north along the main street, in the direction of Strathyre. Go past the Dreadnought Hotel and watch for a park and children's playground on your left. Turn onto the path through the park and follow it across a footbridge over Garbh Uisge.

This path leads through quiet farmland, with the peak of Ben Ledi visible directly ahead (*see* Walk 15). Near the start of the walk, you will see an old burial ground (associated with the clan Buchanan) on a small hillock to your left. A little further on you pass the remains of a Roman fort on your right (all that remains are the grass-covered walls).

Follow the easy path until you reach the A821. Cross this (carefully) and continue. The most dramatic sections of the Falls are not visible from the route, and to see them you will have to turn onto one of the rough paths through the woods to the right of the track (please avoid disturbing fishermen). Whichever way you choose, continue a little way beyond the Falls: the pleasantest part of the track is through the oakwoods above the Falls.

This section of the track ends at the car park for Ben Ledi. You may wish to continue your walk a little further, following the cycle route to Loch Lubnaig and on towards Strathyre. Otherwise, turn back here and return by the same route.

This is an enjoyable circuit over varying terrain, with a steep climb to a fine viewpoint and a visit to a splendid waterfall. There is a car park at the start of the Bracklinn Falls path, for those who wish to walk that section of the walk on its own. Length: 4½ miles/7km; Height Climbed: 820ft/250m.

O.S. Sheet 57

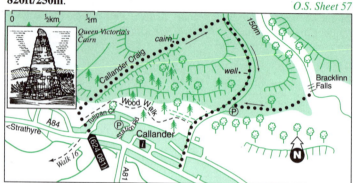

Park in Callander and walk west along the main street (ie, in the direction of Strathyre). When the park opens up to the left watch for Tulipan Crescent cutting back to the right (this is also accessible from the back of the main car park: *see* map). Turn onto this, then left up a tarmac track heading for the woods.

The path splits at the beginning of the slope. Go left, climbing steeply on a well-constructed woodland path. The deciduous wood and abundant wildlife make for pleasant walking.

As you approach the top, the angle of ascent eases and there are fine views of Callander and of the hills to the north and west. The cairn to commemorate Queen Victoria's golden jubilee is right on the summit,

with trees to the right and open hillside on the left.

Continue beyond the cairn on a rough, muddy path; descending to reach a tarred road. Turn right and continue downhill on this quiet, single-track road. Pass the signpost for the Red Well (a natural spring rich in iron) and continue to the car park for the Bracklinn Falls.

The walk to the falls is popular and easy, and the noise of the river, as it leaps over huge blocks of stone in the deep gorge, is tremendous.

Retrace your steps to the road and follow it down to the town. (If you wish to avoid the town centre, a turn to the right at the sign for the Wood Walk will lead you back to Tulipan Crescent.)

Three short waymarked walks in the woods and open land above Loch Venachar, including a steep climb to a viewpoint. Length: ¹/₂-3 *miles/* **1-5km***; Height Climbed:* **150ft/50m***.*

O.S. Sheet 57

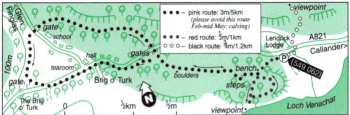

These three walks start from the Woodland Trust's Little Drum car park, a mile east of Brig o' Turk on the A821.

Brig o' Turk Loop (*pink markers*) is the longest route. Start from the information board and follow the path through oak woodland. At a log bench, after the first short climb, turn right. Follow the rough path to a kissing gate, then continue up a small hillock on narrow stone slab steps.

This leads to open ground (muddy in places). Continue until you reach four small boulders across the path, one with a marker on it. Turn right, descending to a wooden platform and a kissing gate by the road.

Cross the road (carefully) to reach another gate. This leads to a wooden walkway through the Brig o' Turk Mires Special Wildlife Site (which used to be the local curling pond). At the end of the walkway go right, as indicated, along a gravel track.

This path ends quite quickly, and is replaced by a grassy track. This leads through a gate then runs downhill, crossing a few small streams, to the single-track road leading to Glen Finglas.

Cross the road and continue along a path between the field and the river. Follow this to a gate, a short way before the road, and turn left before it. When the path reaches the road, cross to the pavement and continue through the village, passing the tearoom.

When the pavement ends, take a footpath which runs beside the road. Go through a kissing gate and return to your outward route.

Little Drum Wood Walk (*red markers*) Start as above, but keep straight on at the bench and continue down to the edge of Loch Venachar, before returning by a different route.

Lendrick Hill (*black markers*) Head east from the car park, by the road. Cross the burn then cross the road (carefully) to reach a pedestrian gate. Follow the steep path beyond this to a wooden bench overlooking the valley. Return the same way.

Walks The Trossachs

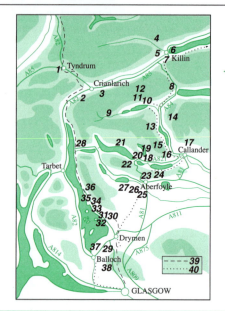

Grades

A+ .... Full walking equipment – including map and compass – and previous hill walking experience essential

A ...... Full walking equipment required

B ...... Strong walking footwear and waterproof clothing required

C ...... Comfortable walking footwear recommended

[**B/C**, etc ...... Split grades mean that there is more than one route described, and the walks are of varying degrees of difficulty.]

NB: Assume each walk increases at least one grade in winter conditions. Hill routes can become extremely treacherous.

Walks The Trossachs

walk	grade	walk	grade
1 Tyndrum Mines	B	**21** Loch Katrine	B
2 An Caisteal	A+	**22** Ben Venue	A
3 Ben More & Stob Binnein	A+	**23** The Highland Boundary Fault Trail	B
4 Allt Dhùin Croisg	B	**24** The Menteith Hills	B
5 Creag Bhuidhe	B	**25** Doon Hill	C
6 The Old Railway	C	**26** Lochan Spling	C
7 Achmore Wood	C	**27** Loch Ard	B
8 Glen Ogle Trail	B	**28** Two Walks at Inversnaid	B
9 Inverlochlarig	B	**29** Duncryne	C
10 Creag an Tuirc	C	**30** Conic Hill	B
11 Kirkton Glen	B	**31** Millennium Forest Trail	C
12 Balquhidder to Ledcharrie	A	**32** Inchcailloch	C
13 Beinn an t-Sidhein	A	**33** Balmaha to Milarrochy	C
14 Glen Ample	A	**34** Cashel	B/C
15 Ben Ledi	A+	**35** Sallochy to Rowardennan	B
16 Callander to Falls of Leny	C	**36** Ben Lomond	A+
17 Callander Crags & Bracklinn Falls	B	**37** Balloch Castle Country Park	C
18 Brig o' Turk Walks	B/C	**38** The Whangie	B
19 Glen Finglas	A	**39** The West Highland Way	
20 Ben A'an	A	**40** The National Cycle Network	

Published by: Hallewell Publications, The Milton, Foss, Pitlochry, Perthshire PH16 5NQ
Printed by: Halcon Printing Ltd, Stonehaven

While every care has been taken in the preparation of this guide, the publishers cannot accept responsibility for any loss, damage or injury resulting from its use.

Glen Finglas is managed by the Woodland Trust (see Walk 18 for other walks). The Mell Trail is a very popular 15-mile loop through the glen. Length: 15 miles/24km; Height Climbed: 1650ft/500m.

O.S. Sheet 57

Start from the Glen Finglas car park, ¹/₂ mile east of the village of Brig o' Turk, on the A821 between Aberfoyle and Callander. A map in the car park shows two routes: a short (blue) loop to a viewpoint and the longer (yellow) Mell Trail.

Walk out of the back of the car park, over a bridge and through a gate. When the path splits, keep left (yellow and blue) climbing steeply. After a short distance, a path cuts back to the right (blue). Continue ahead (yellow) on the clear path which climbs then contours the hill before dropping to join the private road above Glen Finglas Reservoir.

Turn right here along the side of the loch. As you walk along, a few farm tracks cut off but the main road stays by the loch and is perfectly clear, although it changes from tarmac to a good farm track. There are a few gates: leave them as you find them.

After 3 miles/5km the track splits. Go right, up Glen Meann, following the signpost for the Mell Trail and the path to Balquhidder.

From here on, the track circles Meall Cala in a huge loop. A few tracks head off the main track: the first is a track that cuts down to cross the river on the left; the second is a junction just before you reach the path to Balquhidder (go right instead of carrying straight on); the third, the

path to Balquhidder itself. Ignore all of these.

Follow the track up and across the moorland to the highest point of the walk (marked by a cairn). From here there is a pleasant descent down to Glen Finglas. The track then follows the river back down to the reservoir.

*A short, steep, lineal route – one of the most beautiful short hill walks in Scotland. Ben A'an's location, right in the heart of the Trossachs, ensures great views over the surrounding lochs and hills, while its rocky summit lends the walk an air of wilderness. Length: **2¹/₂ miles/4km** (there and back); Height Climbed: **1150ft/350m**.*

O.S. Sheet 57

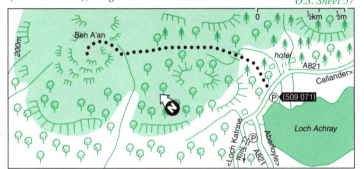

The Ben A'an car park is above Loch Achray on the A821 Aberfoyle to Callander road, about 2 miles west of Brig o' Turk. From Aberfoyle, the road climbs over the Duke's Pass, giving good views of Ben Ledi (*see* Walk 15). The car park, which is clearly marked from the road, can be busy in the summer.

From the car park, cross the road (carefully) and follow the obvious path which leads up through the trees. After a fairly steep ascent the path crosses a bridge. Shortly beyond it flattens out, giving you time to get your breath back. After crossing two more small streams, the path climbs out of the trees and heads for the summit up a series of rocky steps.

Just below the summit, a path branches off to the left. This is the shortest route, but a little scrambling may be required close to the top. The main path follows an easier route, flattening out a little and looping round to the summit, with it's spectacular views of Loch Katrine.

Descend by the same route, taking care with the loose rocks in the higher sections of the walk.

Ben A'an from the path

Loch Katrine is one of the gems of the Trossachs, the scenery and the trips on the SS Sir Walter Scott attracting thousands of visitors each year. This walk is along the private (Water Board) road that runs much of the way round the loch, linking the two ferry piers. It is possible to do lineal walks from either end, but if you wish to make a round trip it is easiest to take the morning ferry (11am) from the east end pier to Stronachlachar and walk back. Length: **13 miles/21km**_; Height Climbed:_ undulating.

O.S. Sheets 56 & 57

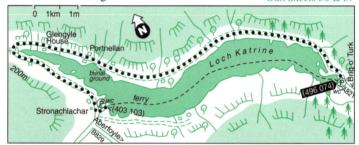

There are car parks at either end of this route. **To reach the east end car park**, take the well-signposted road which turns off the A821 just west of the village of Brig o' Turk. **To reach Stronachlachar**, follow the B829 west from Aberfoyle for about 13 miles.

The private metalled road runs along the north side of the loch and around its west end. There is no doubt about the route, though you should watch out for occasional vehicles. The scenery here is magnificent, and there are interpretative panels at the sites of interest along the way. Although the road climbs quite steeply in places, the walking is generally easy, and there are some

fine waterfalls to be seen.

At the west end of the loch, you will pass Glengyle House, on the site of the building where Rob Roy MacGregor was born (_see_ Introduction). A little to the east of this, you will pass the traditional burial place of the clan MacGregor, on a small island joined to the shore by a causeway.

Clan MacGregor burial island

*One of the classic hill walks in the Trossachs. The summit is imposing, but there is a well-trodden path to the top. Length: **7¹/₂ miles/12km** (there and back); Height Climbed: **2100ft/640m**. For those who wish to extend the walk, there is a possible descent to Loch Ard – though you will have to arrange transport for the far end.*

O.S. Sheet 57

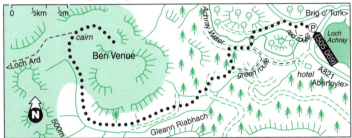

Park in the Ben Venue car park, on the A821 2 miles west of Brig o' Turk. Three waymarked paths start here: this walk follows the blue route.

Walk out of the back of the car park (all walks) on a clear path. At the first junction, keep right (blue/green) and follow the path towards the public road. Just before the road, head left on a private tarred road and follow this until a waymarked path cuts off to the left. Follow this to an arched wooden bridge. Cross this and continue to a junction with a forest road. Turn right, and continue for 200m then turn left onto a clear path which climbs steeply through trees.

When you reach a T-junction, turn right (blue) and climb to join a forestry road. Turn left along this for 150m, then turn right onto a footpath which crosses a small burn.

Climb up to another forestry road, cross it, then continue on a footpath through a felled area, with the forest road through Gleann Riabhach below you. Continue up the glen (ignoring a path crossing the way), passing through more trees and climbing to reach a fence and a stile.

Beyond this the path becomes muddy and less obvious, but it stays to the right of the burn and climbs up past a small waterfall. After a short flat section, the path climbs again to a cairn. This marks the junction of the paths leading to the summit and to Loch Ard (an alternative descent).

From here the path to the top is fairly obvious, though you should take care on steep sections.

Descend to the cairn by the same route. Don't be tempted by alternative descents – the ground is tougher than it looks.

Return by the same route.

This signposted forest walk is one for the geologists, as it includes
information on the Highland Boundary Fault which runs through
this area. Length: **4 miles/6.5km**; *Height Climbed:* **500ft/150m** (add
260ft/80m for climb to viewpoint). *Fine views.*

O.S. Sheet 57

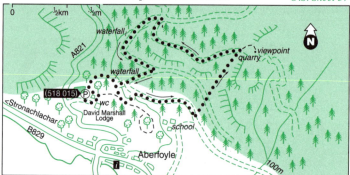

The David Marshall Lodge is just
north of Aberfoyle on the A821.
The Lodge has an interesting Birds
of Prey research station, restaurant,
shops and toilets, and there are
three waymarked walks in the
forest starting from the centre. The
Highland Boundary Fault Trail has
blue waymarkers.

Start directly outside the Lodge
and descend past a children's play
area to reach a burn, just below a
small waterfall.

Turn downstream, ignoring the
first bridge to your left. At the second
bridge, cross the stream to join a
wider forestry track. Turn right along
this, passing above some low wooden
buildings (a residential school).

Shortly after this the walk cuts
off to the left on a narrow footpath

climbing a steep slope. It crosses a
road at one point, but is otherwise
fairly relentless until you reach the
remains of the Lime Craig Quarry
near the top of the hill.

From here, there is a possible short
extension to the walk, to reach the
viewpoint on the summit of the hill
above the quarry. Otherwise, turn
left down a forestry track. When
you reach a four-way junction, take
the forest road which leads down to
the left (part of the National Cycle
Network route), and follow the track
down, past another small waterfall on
your right, to another junction.

Turn right here (signposted) and
you will find yourself back at the
bridge below the first waterfall, from
where it is a short walk back to the
Lodge.

A pleasant lineal walk over a low hill pass, from just east of Aberfoyle to Loch Venachar. Possible extension to Callander on a quiet metalled road. The path is clear, but muddy in places. Length: **4 miles/6.5km** (one way, Braeval to Loch Venachar)*;* **8 miles/13km** (one way, Braeval to Callander)*; Height Climbed:* **600ft/180m.**

O.S. Sheet 57

To reach the start of the walk, drive south from Aberfoyle on the A821, then turn left onto the A81. Shortly after you pass a golf course, you will see Braeval forestry car park on your left.

A broad vehicle track leaves from the back of the car park. Follow this as it leads up through the woods. Take a left at the first junction, and go straight ahead at the second (this is signposted for Callander).

After a steady climb, the forestry road ends and a muddy footpath starts on the other side of a stile. The path continues through trees for about a mile/1.5km to reach another stile. Cross this to leave the trees, emerging into open, bracken-covered ground.

The path crosses a stream and continues to another stile. Cross this and continue, through conifers, to reach the side of a lochan. Follow the path by the lochan until it climbs to join a forestry road (directly opposite, at this point, a short diversion leads up to a viewpoint looking over Loch Venachar to Ben Ledi).

Turn right (downhill) along the forest road. After a few metres a sign marks the start of a path to the left. Turn onto this and descend, through trees, to reach the side of Loch Venachar by a right of way sign.

From here, you can either return by the same route, or follow the quiet road to the right for about 3½ miles/5.5km. This will take you into Callander, from where you can get a bus back to Aberfoyle.

Two short walks from Aberfoyle. **25)** *An easy walk to a wooded hill with a supernatural history. Parking at the walk is limited so it is better to start from Aberfoyle. Length:* **2 miles/3km***; Height Climbed:* **200ft/ 60m***.* **26)** *A waymarked forest walk around a small lochan. Length:* **3³/₄ miles/6km***; Height Climbed:* undulating.

O.S. Sheet 57

For both walks, head west from the centre of Aberfoyle. At the junction, keep straight on along the road to Stronachlachar. Immediately beyond the junction, turn left on a minor road crossing a small bridge.

Walk 25) Follow the road past the church and go round a bend to reach a small parking place with a sign for the 'Doon Hill Fairy Trail'. Walk on along the private road for about 300m to reach a sign for a path to your left.

A 17th-century local minister, Robert Kirk, wrote a book about the area's fairies. Angered by his betrayal, they are said to have captured him and imprisoned his spirit in a pine at the top of Doon Hill.

The path winds up through the woods then leads up some rough steps to the hilltop. At the top, there is a small clearing with a particularly imposing Scots pine.

There is an arrow pointing down to the left. The path leads round the side of the hill, cuts away to the right, then finally comes down to meet a forestry road. Turn left along this, as shown, to return to the private road.

Walk 26) A short way beyond the bridge, turn right at the sign for Inchrie Castle. This road leaves the houses and becomes a forest track. Continue along this until you reach a clear four-way junction.

Turn right (yellow marker) and descend to a junction just beyond a small burn. Here you have a choice, with two paths marked by yellow posts. The right-hand path climbs to a viewpoint; the other follows the pleasant wooded shore of the lochan. They rejoin after a short distance.

The track swings away from the lochan to reach a junction. Turn left, then left again at the next junction. The broad track then leads back, past the lochan, to the original track.

The Forestry Commission have laid out three waymarked walks through the woods by Loch Ard. This walk follows sections of two of the routes to form a circuit, starting by the loch then climbing to a fine viewpoint.
Length: **4 miles/6.5km***; Height Climbed:* **300ft/90m.**

O.S. Sheet 57

From Aberfoyle, it is possible either to walk or drive to the start of these walks (at Milton car park). If you are walking, follow Walk 26 to reach the link path shown on the map.

To reach the car park, drive west from Aberfoyle on the B829 for a mile. Just before a small converted mill, to the left of the road, a small road cuts left and crosses the river. Follow the signs for Milton car park.

Three routes are signposted from the car park. For this walk, follow the posts for the red walk back down the entrance road. At a junction by a house entrance turn left (red marker) and follow a clear track which quickly joins the side of Loch Ard.

Continue along this pleasant path until it splits. At this point ignore the yellow/red markers to the left and keep straight on, along the loch side. The route is perfectly clear, with fine views of the loch and the peak of Ben Lomond beyond. There is one

possible diversion after about a mile/ 1.5km, where, at the end of a bay, a narrow path heads off to the right around a wooded promontory. This is a pleasant extension and rejoins the main track in a short distance.

Continue to a waymarked three-way junction, with a cycle route continuing ahead, and the red route cutting up and back to the left.

Turn on to this and follow the clear track through the trees. Ignore the first track cutting off to the right and continue to a further waymarked junction (about a mile/1.5km after leaving the loch side).

Turn right here (yellow marker) and climb through a felled area to reach a viewpoint (the Wallace Monument is visible in the valley to the east) then drop down the slope beyond to reach a further junction with a clear forest track. Turn left along this (yellow marker) to return to the car park.

28 Two Walks at Inversnaid _____ B

Two short loops through woodland on the slopes above Loch Lomond.
Fine views from both. **A)** *Length:* **2¹/₄ miles/3.5km**; *Height Climbed:*
500ft/150m; **B)** *Length:* **2 miles/3km**; *Height Climbed:* **500ft/150m**.

To reach Inversnaid, drive 11 miles
west from Aberfoyle on the B829,
then turn left onto the minor road
which ends at the hotel and car park
by the side of Loch Lomond. The
West Highland Way runs through
here (*see* Walk 39) and the two walks
described start along its route.

Walk A) Turn north (right, as you
look at the loch) and follow the shore
path through the pleasant woodland
of Inversnaid Nature Reserve. The
path passes an old boathouse. Just
beyond this a sign points right for the
RSPB Trail.

The trail climbs through oakwood
to the right of a burn, then crosses the
burn to reach a fine viewpoint before
dropping back to the lochside.

Either return from this point or
continue northwards for a short way
to reach the signposted 'Rob Roy's
Cave'. The path is pleasant, but the
cave itself is difficult and dangerous
to find amongst the slippery, tumbled
rocks above the loch.

Walk B) Turn south, across the
face of the hotel, and climb steps
to cross the bridge over the Arklet

O.S. Sheet 56

Water. Beyond the bridge the path
splits. Keep left. At the next junction
keep left again and climb the steep
path above the burn.

As the path approaches the upper
car park there is a junction. Go right,
descending, watching for a sign for
the viewpoint. Make a diversion
(left) to see the view (path damp),
then return to the junction and follow
the path downhill, back to the start.

1 *The Cobbler (Ben Arthur)* 2 *Beinn Narnain* 3 *Beinn Ime* 4 *Beinn Chorranach* 5 *Ben Vane* 6 *Tarbet*
7 *Ben Vorlich* 8 *Feed pipes from Loch Sloy to power station*

A short, easy lineal climb to a low summit, giving excellent views of Loch Lomond and the surrounding hills. The path can be muddy: make sure you wear appropriate footwear. Length: **²/₃-1¹/₂ miles/1-2.5km** (there and back)*; Height Climbed:* **260ft/80m.**

O.S. Sheet 56

The wooded hill of Duncryne is an obvious landmark behind the village of Gartocharn (3 miles north of Balloch on the A811). There is limited parking at the start of the climb (half a mile down a minor road from the village centre), but if this is full, park outside the Village Hall (opposite the Hungry Monk).

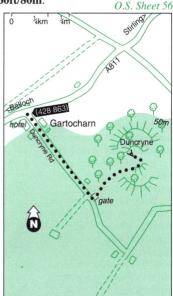

Cross the road. Walk left, past the hotel and turn right up Duncryne Road. Follow this for half a mile/ 1km until, just past Duncryne Cott., there is a parking area, a wood and a gate on your left. There are various signs here, asking you not to drop litter and to stay on the path.

Follow the path through the woods and across a brief, muddy stretch of farmland. Go through another gate (or, strangely, round it: the fence is missing) and follow the lower path as it curves round the south face of the hill. The path snakes up to the summit, and a trig point.

The views from the top are tremendous. The view north, over

Loch Lomond, is shown below. Look also for the Campsie Fells and Fintry Hills to the east.

Return by the same route.

1 *Beinn Eich* 2 *Creinch* 3 *Doune Hill* 4 *Beinn Dubh* 5 *Torrinch* 6 *Beinn Bhreac* 7 *Inchcailloch*
8 *Ben Lomond* 9 *Craigie Fort*

*Three walks starting from Balmaha. **30)** A very pleasant hill walk on good paths, passing through varied countryside. Great views, though path can be busy in the summer. **NB:** possible limits to access during lambing season; check signs locally. Length: up to **5 miles/8km**; Height Climbed: **1150ft/350m**. **31)** A fine short walk through woodland and by the shore of the loch. Features a short climb to a fine viewpoint. Length: **1 mile/1.5km**; Height Climbed: **130ft/40m**. **32)** A selection of paths around a small wooded island, reached by a ferry. Length: **1¹/₂ miles/2.5km**; Height Climbed: **250ft/75m**.*

O.S. Sheets 56 & 57

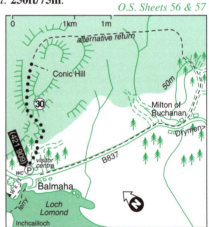

To reach Balmaha, on the shore of Loch Lomond, drive 4 miles west of Drymen on the B837. Park in the large car park in the middle of the village, where there is an information centre.

Walk 30) At the back of the car park, there are signs for short forestry walks, the Conic Hill walk, and the West Highland Way. Start the walk by following the West Highland Way signs to the right, along a wide track.

After a few hundred metres, you will see a clear marker

View from Walk 31: 1 *Inchfad* **2** *Bucinch* **3** *Beinn Eich* **4** *Doune Hill* **5** *Glen Luss*
6 *Inchlonaig* **7** *Beinn Dubh* **8** *Beinn Bhreac* **9** *Ben Lomond*

directing you to the left, up the side of a small burn. Follow the narrowing path as it winds up and onto the shoulder of the hill (passing a kissing gate and a viewpoint on the way).

From here the path climbs straight up, and goes round the northern side of the hill (just below the summit). This top section can be quite slippery, as the path occasionally fades while going over grassy ground. Near the top, there is an alternative path (to the right) that allows you to visit the summit and get good views over Loch Lomond.

For the quickest return from the top of the hill, simply retrace your steps. If you wish to extend your walk, follow the path to the left as it begins a slow descent. Follow the path across a bridge, then a stile, then over a grassy section, keeping a fence on your left. At the end of the fence, cross a large stile and follow the path through the woods.

This leads on to a forestry road. Follow this in the same direction. When it splits, take the right-hand path. Follow this until you reach another junction: take a right, and follow the road down to Milton of Buchanan. From here, it is just less than a mile back to Balmaha along the road.

Walk 31) At the back of the car park, turn left along the clear track through the woods and down to the public road. Cross over and continue on the clear track by the lochside.

When the track reaches the pier at the end of the headland a path heads up the slope to the right, signposted for the walk. Follow this to the top of the hill, from where there is a splendid view of the loch (*see opposite page*).

Follow the path down the far side of the hill to return to the loch shore. Turn left along the rough shoreline path to return to the start.

Walk 32) Inchcailloch is a wooded island, a little under a mile in length, just off the shore at Balmaha. It is now owned by Scottish Natural Heritage and maintained as a nature reserve. Access to the island is by passenger ferry from the MacFarlane Boatyard at Balmaha. The ferry runs on demand (www.balmahaboatyard.co.uk).

Paths are laid out through the woods on the island, climbing to a viewpoint and passing the sandy bay at Port Bawn and the old graveyard. The latter is a reminder of the island's long history as a religious site, which dates back to the 8th century.

O.S. Sheet 56

33 Balmaha to Milarrochy _____ C

A short, lineal walk through woodland by the side of Loch Lomond, following a section of the West Highland Way and leading to a pleasant sandy bay. Length: 1¹/₂ miles/2.5km (one way); Height Climbed: up to **130ft/40m.** *Possible link with Walk 34.*

Start this walk as for Walk 31. When you reach the pier, you have the choice of either climbing the hill to your right or continuing along the shore. Either way, once the two paths have rejoined beyond the point, continue along the shore to the car park and beach at Milarrochy.

It is possible to continue along the West Highland Way for a further 1¹/₂ miles/2.5km to link with Walk 34. Otherwise, return by the same route.

O.S. Sheet 56

34 Cashel _____ B/C

Three circuits of differing lengths laid out through newly-planted native woodland on a steep slope above Loch Lomond. Excellent views. Length: ³/₄-4 miles/1.1-6.5km; Height Climbed: up to **850ft/260m.**

Cashel is two miles north of Balmaha on the Loch Lomond shore road. There is parking by the buildings at the top of the drive.

This small estate has been bought by the Royal Scottish Forestry Society as a site for regenerating native woodland, and three waymarked routes have been laid out through the new plantations. The shortest is no more than a pleasant stroll; the longest (with its steep ascent) a fairly strenuous hike. In addition to the pleasure of observing the new woodland, all three walks provide fine views over the loch.

O.S. Sheet 56

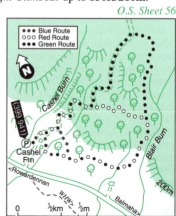

An easy, lineal walk, following a section of the West Highland Way through the woods of the east shore of Loch Lomond. Path clear but muddy in places. Length: **2¹/₄ miles/3.5km** *(one way); Height Climbed: undulating. Possible link with Walk 36.*

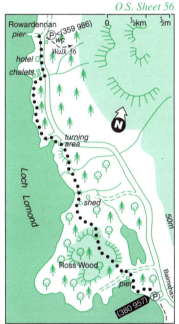

O.S. Sheet 56

To reach Sallochy car park, drive 3 miles north along the minor road which runs from Balmaha up the east side of Loch Lomond. The car park is signposted to the left of the road.

Follow the path marked for the West Highland Way (WHW) over a wooden footbridge and on along the wooded shore. After a short distance the path narrows as it rounds a rocky headland.

Beyond this there is a small bay with a wooden pier. Follow the path around the bay to the University Field Station. Just beyond this there is a junction. Turn right on a small path marked for the WHW. The path leaves the loch and climbs steeply up a wooded hill before descending gradually and passing to the left of a stone shed.

Cross a wooden footbridge in front of a cottage (Mill of Ross) and continue northwards. The path is in no real doubt; crossing a further footbridge and a low hill beyond before dropping to reach a car turning area by a small bay.

Look for the WHW marker to your left and follow a small path, close to the public road, which leads down to the bay. At the end of the bay there is a junction with a vehicle track. Turn left along this. As the track ends,

look for the WHW marker to the right and climb through Scots Pine woods above the loch before dropping down to join the public road by some wooden chalets.

Turn left along the road, passing the Rowardennan Hotel, and continue to the car park by the pier.

Return by the same route.

This beautiful mountain dominates Loch Lomond and is a spectacular landmark for travellers heading north from Glasgow. The path to the summit is quite straightforward, but this is a big mountain and you should be fully equipped. Length: **8 miles/13km** (there and back)*; Height Climbed:* **3150ft/960m***.*

O.S. Sheet 56

To reach the start, take the road from Drymen along the east shore of Loch Lomond. The road turns up beside the Winnoch Hotel and is signposted to Balmaha. It can be very busy in the summer.

Follow the road through Balmaha. After 11 miles you reach the car park at the end of the road – about 300m beyond the Rowardennan Hotel.

The path starts behind the timber toilet building in the trees behind the pier. It climbs up through the trees, muddy in places, and crosses a forestry road. Just beyond the road there is a brief respite when the path levels out, but the climb soon resumes. There are some steep and rocky sections before you emerge from the trees and come through a gate onto the open hillside. This is grazing land for cattle and sheep, and dogs must be kept on a lead beyond the gate.

Another steep climb takes you onto the section of the walk known as 'The Plateau'. It is not, unfortunately, flat, but it does give a steady and gentle ascent to the base of the summit pyramid.

The summit is approached by a series of zig-zags up the steep face and a final traverse along the edge of

Rowardennan Memorial

the summit ridge. The view from the top is spectacular, with Loch Lomond to the west and the Trossachs to the east.

Descend by the same route. You are asked to stay on the path while descending to minimise erosion.

The grounds of Balloch Castle were landscaped by John Buchanan in the 19th century. They are perfect for a casual stroll, and very popular all year round. It is possible to walk anywhere you want, but this route takes you round most of the gardens. Length: **2 miles/3km***; Height Climbed: negligible.*

Drive north through Balloch on the A811. Just before you leave the town, you will see a sign for the Balloch Castle Country Park on your left. Follow the signs into the grounds and park in the main car park.

Take the path just below the car park and – noting the view down to the loch – follow it to the right. This leads you along the top of the gardens and then down the Fairy Glen to the lochside.

The path then leads back along the shore, and you get good views of the loch and up to Balloch Castle (built in 1808 and now housing the visitor centre). Pass the boathouse on your right then look for the site of the original castle on your left. The old castle was moved in the 15th century by the Earl of Lennox to a more secure location on the island of Inchmurrin. You can see the island from the walk. The ruin of the old castle is just to the left of a white house at the west end of the island.

Carry on along the banks of the River Leven, where you can see a variety of boats. Follow the tarmac path up to the left, across a low bridge, which will lead you back to the top of the gardens. If you want to visit the walled gardens, the second

O.S. Sheet 56

path on your left, after crossing the bridge, is the easiest route. As you reach the top of the park, follow the path round to the left, and return to the start of the walk, visiting the castle on the way.

The Whangie is a classic short walk which has been popular since Victorian times. Auchineden Hill appears quite unremarkable from the road, but the outcrops at the back of the hill are surprising and spectacular. Length: **3 miles/5km** *(there and back); Height Climbed:* **500ft/150m**.

O.S. Sheet 64

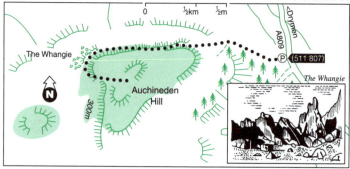

The large car park at the start of this walk is at the east end of Auchineden Hill, about 6 miles south of Drymen on the A809. Please note the signpost at the start of the path, asking you to keep to the illustrated route in order to avoid erosion.

Follow the path as it leads over an unusual stone stile in a wall and on up a grassy slope beyond. As you reach the end of the forest on your left, you will see a well-trodden path cutting up and around a stile: ignore this and follow the path which contours around the hill.

As you reach the west side of the hill, and the path begins to turn southwards, you need to climb up a small stone step. Shortly after this, the path splits. Take the lower path to the right.

Follow the path until you reach The Whangie itself. There are two paths: one which leads through the crags and another which runs around the bottom of them. Both paths are quite safe. Legend has it that this slash in the hillside was caused by the Devil's tail, but there is also a more rational geological explanation.

As you leave the other end of the rocky gully, follow the path to the left and up a short steep section to reach the summit of Auchineden Hill. There are splendid views: east to the Campsie Fells and north to the hills around Loch Lomond (*see* Walk 29 for an annotated illustration of a similar view).

Return by the same route.

The oldest and most popular of Scotland's waymarked, long-distance footpaths. A large section of the West Highland Way runs through this area, and it can be walked in part or in whole. Short sections of the Way appear in this guide as parts of other routes. The route can be joined in numerous places (see individual walks).

The West Highland Way is 95 miles/152km long; running north from Milngavie, near Glasgow, to Fort William. The route (officially opened in 1980) makes use of old drove roads, military roads and disused railways, and passes through some of Scotland's most stunning scenery.

In this area, the Way passes through Drymen, crosses Conic Hill (*see* Walk 30) runs north along the shore of Loch Lomond (Walks 31,33,35,28) then continues past Crianlarich and Tyndrum (Walk 1) before heading north across Rannoch Moor (*see* companion volumes *Walks Oban & North Argyll* and *Walks Fort William & District*).

A number of detailed guides to the route are available, and the waymarking makes it comparatively easy to follow. In addition, **www. west-highland-way.co.uk** carries useful background information and advice, as well as providing up to date information on any path diversions, accommodation, etc.

The route can be walked in either direction, but if you are planning to follow it for any distance it is recommended that you walk south to north – ie, with the sun and the prevailing wind at your back.

O.S. Sheets 50,56,57 & 64

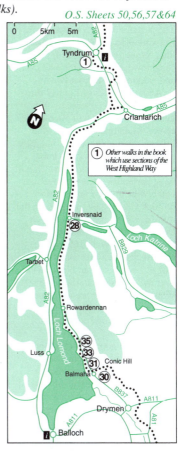

The National Cycle Network, opened in 2000, covers several thousand miles and is still expanding. Route 7 (Carlisle to Inverness) passes through this area. This will be of particular interest to cyclists, but the off-road sections are also useful for walkers, and some of them are used in routes in this guide.

The purpose of the National Cycle Network is to make use of old railway lines, quiet roads, forestry tracks and canal towpaths to provide safe cycling and walking throughout Britain.

About 60 miles of Route 7 runs through the area covered by this guide, and walkers will often come across the signposts. Much of it follows quiet public roads, but there are off-road sections (with good surfaces and signposting) which will be of particular interest to walkers: notably the disused railway line through Glen Ogle (*see* Walk 8); the route down the west side of Loch Lubnaig, between Strathyre and Callander (*see* Walk 16); and the road/track which runs along the south side of Loch Venachar before winding over the hill to reach Aberfoyle (*see* Walk 24). Walkers are welcome on these sections, though you are asked to be aware of (and courteous to) passing cyclists.

There is a good leaflet, showing the route, available from Tourist Information Centres (*see* map at front of book). Alternatively, useful information (including route maps) is available at www.sustrans.org.uk

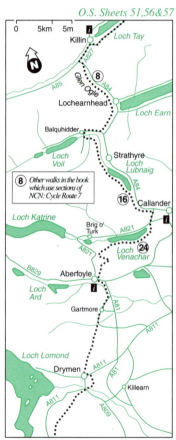

O.S. Sheets 51,56&57

8 Other walks in the book which use sections of NCN: Cycle Route 7